Guidance Program
Development

Guidance Program Development

By

DANIEL L. BALLAST, Ed.D.

Supervisor of Guidance Services
Grand Rapids Public Schools
Grand Rapids, Michigan

and

RONALD L. SHOEMAKER, M.A.

Director of Guidance and Special Services
Godwin Heights Public Schools
Wyoming, Michigan

CHARLES C THOMAS • PUBLISHER

Springfield • Illinois • U.S.A.

Published and Distributed Throughout the World by
CHARLES C THOMAS • PUBLISHER
Bannerstone House
301-327 East Lawrence Avenue, Springfield, Illinois, U.S.A.

© *1978, by* CHARLES C THOMAS • PUBLISHER
ISBN 0-398-03744-2
Library of Congress Catalog Card Number: 77-14438

With THOMAS BOOKS *careful attention is given to all details of*
manufacturing and design. It is the Publisher's desire to present books that
are satisfactory as to their physical qualities and artistic possibilities and
appropriate for their particular use. THOMAS BOOKS *will be true to those*
laws of quality that assure a good name and good will.

Printed in the United States of America
R-1

Library of Congress Cataloging in Publication Data
Ballast, Daniel L
    Guidance program development.

    Bibliography: p.
    Includes index.
    1. Personnel service in education--United States.
I. Shoemaker, Ronald L., joint author. II. Title.
LB1027.5.B25   371.4′0973   77-14438
ISBN 0-398-03744-2

*To students everywhere and the
school counselors who serve them.*

PREFACE

SINCE the National Defense Education Act was passed by Congress in 1958, phenomenal growth in the number of professional guidance and counseling personnel has occurred. The growth in number, however, has not been accompanied with agreement as to what the role or functions of the school counselor should be. Expectations of school counselors vary significantly among teachers, administrators, students, community agency personnel, business personnel, and even among counselors. Without a well-defined role, school counselors have been compelled to respond to crises and to the demands of the moment. In addition, there has been strong criticism and a sense of disappointment in the ability of guidance to meet the expectations and needs of young people.

The financial condition of many school districts is necessitating a critical examination of many areas — including guidance and counseling. One of the basic questions being asked is, "Are school counselors necessary?" Most school districts must rely on economic or personality considerations in answering this question.

The intent of this book is to demonstrate to superintendents, supervisors and directors of guidance, practicing counselors, counselor educators, counselor candidates, school principals, and others that the answer to this question should be found within a school or school district through systematic guidance program development based on the identified needs of students. Direction, problems, rewards, and pitfalls are highlighted as the authors cull from their own experiences with program development.

INTRODUCTION

THE current situation in which guidance in the United States finds itself is created by many far-ranging expectations of school counselors and accentuated by the budget realities of most school districts. Counselors are being pushed and pulled in many directions simultaneously. Many of these expectations and problems in the world of education come from opposite ends of the continuum. Counselors are expected by various publics to have the following abilities:

Be skillful in group counseling as well as individual counseling.

Be educators and, at the same time, mental health workers.

Have allegience to the student and also to the institution of the school.

Deal with concerns of individual students while being responsible to provide guidance for from 250 to 700 or more students.

Be ready to respond to crises and still initiate preventive activities.

Work with students having personal or adjustment concerns and also perform career guidance activities.

Work alone and also be part of a department with common goals and functions.

Do what the building administrator requests and also perform planned guidance activities.

Know all assigned students personally and still manage a guidance program which affects all students indirectly.

Help students make long-range plans and also handle

the day-to-day crises and problems in the school.
Be professional counselors as well as handle the volumes
of paperwork.
Assist students to make decisions and also to recruit
students for programs.

In addition to these varying expectations, the difficulties
of declining enrollments and austerity budgets are resulting in the elimination of counseling positions. The
survival of counselors may well be at stake. How can a
school or school district respond effectively to these problems?

One answer to the dilemma in which guidance finds
itself is systematic program development based on the
needs of students. This book presents one process for systematically developing a balanced, comprehensive guidance program. A cookbook-style, step-by-step approach is
used to help schools and school districts put together a
balanced comprehensive program related directly to the
needs of students. The book is limited to program development and does not focus extensively on guidance and
counseling techniques, delivery systems, or evaluation.

ACKNOWLEDGMENTS

GRATEFUL acknowledgment is made to Gloria Graber, Peggy Mahaney, and Roland (Bud) Vashaw, mostly for their friendship and encouragement, but also for reading the rough draft manuscript of this book and making valuable critical comments and suggestions.

D.L.B.
R.L.S.

CONTENTS

Guidance Program
Development

Chapter One

WHAT SHOULD GUIDANCE BE?

M UCH has been written about the current situation of guidance and the role of the school counselor. Little, however, has been written about guidance program development. The time has arrived to do something tangible and practical to move beyond criticisms and the never-ending debate regarding the role of the school counselor. It is time to develop, publish, and deliver balanced comprehensive guidance programs in schools and school districts. In developing a guidance program, the key elements to produce are the following:

Services related to the guidance needs of all students.
A guidance calendar.
Departmental purpose and direction.
Guidance priorities with direct counselor involvement.
A written counselor job description.
Services directly related to guidance.
A program in printed form.
A system for feedback.
A balanced program.
A climate for new ideas and programs.

Services Related to the Guidance Needs of all Students

School counselors should deliver services aimed directly at meeting the guidance needs of all students assigned to them. In order to do this, guidance needs must be systematically identified and systematically programmed. School counselors will then have the opportunity to put their professional skills and caring approach into action with a basic level of services available and delivered to all students.

A Guidance Calendar

School counselors should have a calendar of activities. The calendar is a week-by-week chronological listing of activities initiated by counselors. The use of a guidance calendar helps to appropriately space activities, avoiding an overload during certain times of the school year. In addition, a calendar insures that particular needs of students are attended to at the time of the year when the need is most compelling and that all activities related to satisfying the needs of young people are completed.

Departmental Purpose and Direction

Counselors should have purpose and direction in activities they perform. Their day-to-day activities should be focused toward the attainment of clearly stated student outcomes. It is necessary that counselors be perceived as members of a department with collective purpose and direction rather than as several persons with the same title acting independently.

Guidance Priorities with Direct Counselor Involvement

Counselors should have direct involvement in determining their priorities. Counselor involvement will result in commitment to developing and carrying out activities which will maintain the priorities. These priorities will help lead to an employment situation that is manageable and one in which counselors are comfortable with the expectations of students, parents, and fellow educators. A manageable job is one in which the counselor knows what has to be done, when it has to be done, and has the skills and time to perform the tasks effectively.

A Written Counselor Job Description

Counselors should have student-oriented job descriptions which describe responsibilities and functions that will lead to the achievement of clearly-stated student outcomes. The job description should be balanced between responsibilities related to the generally accepted areas of personal-social, educational, and career outcomes for students. These areas should be infused with the guidance goal areas of self-understanding, decision-making, interpersonal relations, and educational and vocational development.

Services Directly Related to Guidance

Services that counselors deliver should be directly related to guidance. This requires making distinctions between that which necessitates professional counselor involvement and that which is clerical and assigning personnel accordingly. Distinctions between administrative, curricular, and guidance functions are also required. Counselors should function in areas which utilize their unique professional skills.

A Program in Printed Form

The guidance program should be in a printed form and, thus, easily communicated as a recognizable guidance program. It should be an organized program, on paper, and under one cover. A written program assists students, staff, and parents to understand what counselors do and why they do what they do. In addition, a written program will be invaluable for counselors in managing their time and fulfilling their responsibilities.

A System for Feedback

A process should exist for insuring regular feedback from patrons of the school. Follow-up studies, evaluation questionnaires, interviews, and needs surveys are tools that can only be effective if responded to and used systematically.

A Balanced Program

Counselors should be able to resist the constant pressure to emphasize one aspect of a guidance program over another. A guidance program should be balanced evenly between assisting students with personal-social, educational, and career needs. Plus, the guidance goal areas of self-understanding, decision-making, interpersonal relations, and educational and vocational development should be represented in these student need areas. Another critical aspect of a balanced program is an equal emphasis on the freedom and ability to respond to needs as they arise and on the necessity of taking initiative in satisfying the developmental needs of all students.

A Climate for New Ideas and Programs

The condition of a guidance program should be such that new ideas and programs can be systematically evaluated and accepted in whole, in part, or rejected. This systematic evaluation is based on whether the idea or program will serve to assist counselors to achieve guidance program outcomes.

What Is Program Development?

Program development is a systematic process which

identifies, prioritizes, and provides tools for satisfying the perceived needs and expectations of students. The process includes the following:

Identifying guidance departmental needs.
Generating support for program development.
Establishing departmental leadership.
Preparing the proposal for program development.
Involving key decision makers.
Identifying current services and activities.
Developing tools for the assessment of student needs.
Administration of needs surveys.
Tabulating the results of needs surveys.
Identifying priority needs survey items.
Interpreting the results of the needs surveys.
Developing student outcome statements.
Determination of counselor activities designed to reach student outcomes and integrated with current activities and services.
Identification of timelines and materials.
Development of a guidance calendar including individual counselor responsibilities.
Organizing the guidance program handbook.

Chapter Two

GETTING STARTED: AN ACTION APPROACH

As counselors become convinced that guidance program development is necessary, they may discover resistance to the idea or to actions designed to bring about needed program improvement. Resistance may come from members of the guidance department itself or from others. The resistance may be in subtle ways or may actually become active attempts to stop progress toward program development.

Resistance to Program Development

Several kinds of resistance may occur even before actual program development begins:

The desire to keep things the way they are is a subtle but very powerful phenomenon. The day-to-day demands placed on guidance personnel may make the prospect of program development seem overwhelming. During the initial stages of new program development, the expectations that students, parents, teachers, and administrators have of counselors continue with the same intensity or may even increase. Pressure to keep counselors doing what they always have done may be intense. Related to the pressure of day-to-day demands is the expectation of students, teachers, and administrators that counselors remain in their offices ready to respond when a problem arises. A developed program will require that counselors leave their offices to deliver some services in order to provide an action program for all rather than reactive guidance to only a few.

Building administrators may prefer to avoid direct and intensive involvement in program development because a clear-cut differentiation between what is guidance and what is administrative may occur during program development. As a result, some administrators will give verbal support to guidance program development; however, they may observe it from a distance with the intent that they will ultimately determine what the guidance program will be. This lack of commitment can seriously impede the delivery of the program developed by the guidance staff.

The training of counselors may inhibit their willingness to initiate guidance activities. Counselors are accustomed to being response oriented in fulfilling or carrying out what they have learned in their training. Program development may be perceived as incompatible with this posture and training. Program development will, however, enhance the response function of counselors because of the credibility gained from taking the initiative to help satisfy the identified needs of students.

High pupil-counselor ratios may promote within the guidance staff a futile feeling of "What's the use?" As pupil-counselor ratios increase, it is more difficult for a guidance staff to initiate a guidance program. Guidance program development can, however, articulate the student needs that a guidance staff can attend to no matter what the pupil-counselor ratio. Pupil-counselor ratio must be an important consideration when planning the scope of the counselor's responsibilities. Program development can also act as a springboard to demonstrate the necessity of improved staffing.

In large school districts, the task of program development can appear awesome. One way to make the task more manageable is to begin program development by concentrating on one or a few school buildings at each of the various levels, elementary and secondary. This is best accomplished if there is a feeder school relationship among those involved.

Resistance to Completing Program Development

There will be several roadblocks which will tend to inhibit program completion:

The need for visibility and public relations is frequently so great that there may be a temptation to put disproportionate energy into certain areas of a guidance program. For example, career centers, peer counseling centers, college counseling, and orientation often become ends in themselves. These efforts do indeed have a very positive effect on guidance patrons, but the effect often is narrow in scope. The guidance department may be perceived as detached from these visible efforts or as a fractionalized department going in many directions at the same time.

It may be an equal temptation to stop program development after current guidance department activities have been identified and have assumed program outcomes. The result of this limited program development becomes only a well-organized status quo.

Getting bogged down in developing a statement of purpose is another potential roadblock. Statements of purpose are necessary, but such statements can be written with less philosophical hassle after the process of program development is well underway. The process a guidance department goes through to identify current services and activities, to identify student needs, and to develop outcome statements and purpose activities will assist the department to define its purpose. To begin the process of program development with such a difficult task could cause problems from which it may be difficult to recover. A statement of purpose can more easily be written at the end of the first year of program development.

Resistance to completing program development can be

overcome by establishing a program development calendar which consists of major activities and timelines. The major activities are listed on page 7.

Organizing Within the Guidance Department for Program Development

A comprehensive guidance program that has as its goal the serving of all students with the same level of services must involve an entire guidance department. In the event only one counselor or one administrator in a building or school district is committed to the need for systematic program improvement, the first task of that person is to establish the fact that improvement is necessary and to get the involvement and commitment of the majority of the counselors within the guidance department. A word of caution: make certain that appropriate administrators are informed of all activities designed to assist in organizing the guidance department for program development.

Generating Support for Program Development Within the Guidance Department

Administer the *Baseline Questionnaire* on page 14 to all of the counselors in each building within the school district. Completing the *Baseline Questionnaire* will help establish the need for guidance program development. Results of the *Baseline Questionnaire* may be tabulated by utilizing the *Tally Form* on page 15. Compute the percentage of responses to each item of the questionnaire. Any NO answer may indicate one or all of the following programmatic needs:

ITEM   *NEED*
1.   To systematically determine student needs.
2.   To find ways to serve all students.
3.   To establish a guidance calendar of activities

which can be communicated to students, parents, and staff.

4. To develop direction related to satisfying identified student needs.

5. To have counselors directly and systematically involved in determining the priorities of the guidance department so they know the dimensions of their jobs.

6. To develop a job description which relates responsibilities to student outcomes.

7. To devote staff energy and time in proportion to the student needs.

8. To develop a program which is balanced and explainable in written form.

9. To organize a two-way communications strategy within the school community.

10. To establish criteria for evaluating new ideas, programs, and materials.

List identified guidance department needs:

1.

2.

3.

4.

5.

6.

7.

8.

9.

10.

These needs will be used to validate the need for guidance program development when presented to the school district's key decision makers.

Leadership Strategies Where No Formal Leadership Exists

In many school buildings and school districts, formal

guidance leadership exists in the form of a supervisor, director, head counselor, or department chairperson. Where such leadership exists, forming the organization for program development will be greatly simplified. In many school districts, however, formal guidance leadership does not exist. Where no formal leadership exists, the following approach for program development may be used:

1. Request counselors throughout the district to attend a meeting in order to review the results of the *Baseline Questionnaire.*
2. Agree to hold regular meetings, at least one per month.
3. The guidance staff should appoint a chairperson from within the department (rotating chairpersons could be considered).
4. In multiple staff buildings, each building should appoint a member of the guidance staff to serve on a steering committee. This steering committee should agree to meet regularly and frequently and to give feedback and progress reports to the total department at least monthly.
5. The steering committee should plan procedural steps and establish timelines. Structure the plan in proposal form to be presented to key decision-makers within the school district. Chapters Three, Four, and Five discuss guidelines for proposal development.
6. Present the proposal to the entire guidance department for refinement and approval.

The Proposal for Guidance Program Development

Writing the Proposal

The proposal should state in precise and systematic terms the process which the guidance department is willing to pursue. It should also state the need for guidance program development.

The proposal contains many ingredients. It is important that the proposal reflects the current condition of the guidance department as measured by the *Baseline Questionnaire*. In order to indicate the direction the guidance department would like to go, consideration should be

---

BASELINE QUESTIONNAIRE

1. Yes No   Are the services you deliver designed to meet the systematically identified needs of students?

2. Yes No   Do you think that, basically, you are serving all students assigned to you with the same level of services?

3. Yes No   Do you follow a predetermined calendar of activities which is known to all of your publics?

4. Yes No   Are your activities directly related to the achievement of written student outcomes?

5. Yes No   Are you directly involved in determining which of your activities are more important than others so that your job is manageable?

6. Yes No   Do you have a job description that clearly describes responsibilities related to the achievement of student outcomes?

7. Yes No   Would you say that almost all of your activities are related directly to guidance?

8. Yes No   Do you have a written comprehensive program which is balanced between personal-social, educational, and career concerns?

9. Yes No   Does your department have a systematic way of obtaining and responding to feedback from patrons of the school?

10. Yes No   Do you have criteria against which you evaluate new ideas, programs, or materials?

given to the possibility of including the following information in the proposal:

1. Results of the *Baseline Questionnaire* identifying the need for systematic program development.
2. The process the guidance department plans to follow in outline form (*see* page 7). These steps include developing and administering needs surveys, tabulating results, identifying needs, developing student outcome statements, determining activities needed to reach student outcomes, and putting the program on paper.

BASELINE QUESTIONNAIRE
Tally Form

Question	"No" RESPONSES	Percentage "No" Responses
1.		
2.		
3.		
4.		
5.		
6.		
7.		
8.		
9.		
10.		

3. Time needed to complete program development. Using the activities listed on page 7, plan activities over one school year.
4. A proposed working schedule indicating the times that the steering committee would like to meet.
5. A request for involvement and support of key decision makers in program development, along with a commitment to the delivery of the completed guidance program.

Involving Key Decision Makers

It is imperative the proposal be presented for approval to the key decision makers in a school building and/or school district. A guidance department could independently develop a complete guidance program; however, the risk is high that implementation will not occur without the involvement and support of administrators. Because some administrators may view program development from a distance, the guidance department may want to take the initiative to communicate with administrators throughout the entire process of program development.

IDENTIFYING KEY DECISION MAKERS. Identify the decision makers to whom the guidance proposal should be presented. This may be the principal, a director, assistant superintendent, or superintendent. In a large school district, the guidance chairperson or formal leadership should arrange to attend a principals' meeting in order to present the guidance proposal.

PRESENTING THE PROPOSAL. Involved key decision makers should receive a copy of the proposal in advance of its presentation to them. The reasons for presenting the proposal to the key administrators should be clearly stated to gain their interest, approval, and support. Stress that support already is generated in the guidance department for beginning the program development process. Then review the events which led to the writing of the proposal.

Be prepared to be questioned several times during the presentation. In addition to asking for clarification, administrators may be resistant:

Question: "But counselors are so busy right now!"

Answer: "Yes, but we want these activities to be organized so as to reach clearly defined outcomes."

Question: "Why change a good thing?"

Answer: "If it is a good thing, how can we make it better?"

Question: "Counselors are not spending enough time with students now!"

Answer: "We believe that one result of program development will be a dramatic increase in counselor visibility to, and contact with, students because all students will be receiving assistance in a systematic way."

After the questions and proposal presentation, a decision should be solicited from administrators granting permission to proceed with program development as outlined.

Identifying Current Services and Activities

Counselors in all guidance departments are already performing activities which focus on many student needs. Usually, however, these tasks and needs are not described in writing. Where a staff begins in program development is very important. When a guidance department begins program development by surveying student needs, the implication may be that the department is not focusing on student needs. This, of course, is not true. Such implications can lead to subtle resistance among counselors to systematic program development. It is important to begin with the services and activities that counselors are currently providing. Time spent in identifying current services and activities will be well worth the effort and should provide additional motivation for those involved in the process.

Current Services

The first task of the Guidance Steering Committee is to identify all current services being delivered by the guidance department. It is important to divide current services into smaller segments. For example, counselors may describe their current activities as consulting, coordinating, and counseling. Each of these broad categories, however, can be divided into smaller segments. As each smaller segment, or service, is identified, it should be described. Elementary, middle, and high school counselors differ in the delivery and emphasis of certain services. The steering committee can review these services, add or delete items, and change the descriptions to describe the services as they are currently being delivered. After this task has been completed, transfer the information to the top portion of a *Current Service Form* as shown on page 20. The following services are generally delivered by most guidance departments (the definitions will be different depending on whether the elementary, middle, or high school guidance program is being examined):

ARTICULATION SERVICE. The counselor initiates and carries out activities in "feeder schools" to prepare students for movement from elementary to middle and/or from middle to senior high school.

ORIENTATION SERVICE. The counselor initiates and carries out activities after the beginning of the school year to assist students in adjusting to the new school environment.

FOLLOW-UP SERVICE. The counselor contacts students suspended from school and those students having academic difficulty and attempts to resolve concerns. The counselor may also survey former students in order to obtain feedback regarding their impressions of curriculum and services.

SPECIAL NEEDS SERVICE. The counselor identifies students requiring special school services. The counselor serves on screening committees for special programs, and facilitates contact with, and delivery of, special services to students with identified needs.

COUNSELING SERVICE. The counselor provides an atmosphere within which students feel free to express ideas, feelings, concerns, and interests. Students are then able to examine decisions related to self, education, career, and relationships with others, individually or in groups.

INFORMATION SERVICE. The counselor accumulates, organizes, and disseminates information needed by students in order to make personal, educational, and career decisions.

REFERRAL SERVICE. The counselor refers students and/or parents to an appropriate community or school resource when the need is beyond the range of counselor training or time limitations. When appropriate, the counselor facilitates contact with community resources. The counselor also serves as the school contact person for agencies working with students.

STAFF CONSULTANT SERVICE. The counselor provides staff consultant services by providing information and consulting with staff regarding students. Case conferences are organized and directed when appropriate. The counselor also interprets pupil needs and concerns to staff.

TESTING SERVICE. The counselor coordinates the testing program within the school and interprets test results to faculty, students, and parents.

COURSE SELECTION SERVICE. The counselor assists students and parents in making decisions regarding course selection and programs of study.

POST-HIGH SCHOOL PLANNING AND PLACEMENT SERVICE. The counselor assists students in making post-high school plans such as application to college, technical schools, and

CURRENT SERVICE FORM

SERVICE: Course Selection   GRADES: 9 - 12

DESCRIPTION

The counselor assists students and parents in making decisions regarding course selection and programs of study.

ACTIVITIES

1. Distribute the *Student Program Guide* to students.

2. Assist students in classrooms to select courses.

3. Assist individual students who are having difficulty to select courses and curricular programs.

4. (If appropriate) send course selection materials to data center for keypunching.

5. Resolve scheduling conflicts for individual students.

apprenticeship programs, and financial assistance. The counselor facilitates student contact with representatives of post high school educational institutions and training programs.

JOB PLACEMENT SERVICE. The counselor organizes and operates a job placement service for part-time employment of students and, possibly, for full-time employment after high school.

STUDENT DEVELOPMENT SERVICE. The counselor initiates activities designed to assist students in their personal development, such as decision making, self-awareness, values, and human relations.

Current Activities

After current *services* have been identified, the next step for the steering committee is to identify current *activities* that are being performed to deliver each service. The activities for each service should be put on the bottom portion of a *Current Service Form* in chronological order as in the sample on page 20. Review the materials with the entire guidance staff, and ask for input. When complete, move to the next step in program development: "Student Needs — The Foundation."

Chapter Three

STUDENT NEEDS —
THE FOUNDATION

Identifying Guidance Needs

SCHOOL personnel typically use professional opinions, follow-up data, test results, state and local goals, and objectives of other school districts as a basis for the establishment of program direction. Programs often are developed simply in response to negative criticism and problems which have been identified. Such methods of establishing program direction frequently lack an objectively determined base from which to proceed. On the other hand, the determination of student needs by using a survey or questionnaire identifies needs directly. Students, parents, and staff are asked to respond to specific statements designed to identify student needs. These identified needs are then utilized to help determine the direction of guidance program development.

Needs identification is defined by Kaufman and English (1976): "A need is the gap between what is and what should be . . . A needs assessment is a formal collection of gaps, the placing of gaps in priority order, and selecting the gaps of highest priority for action and resolution. It is a formal process."

In determining the direction of program development, it is important to focus on student needs rather than the problems of the guidance department, the curriculum, the school, or the effectiveness of the present process or program. In summary, needs are related to where a student is and where the student should be, not to where a program should be.

The Needs Survey items have to be related to accepted goals for guidance. In doing this, survey items related to curriculum, discipline, etc. are avoided in favor of items related specifically to guidance. The following Needs Survey items illustrate this point: The first item, "I need to learn how to make better decisions," falls within the purview of guidance. On the other hand, the item, "I need help in mathematics" relates directly to curriculum and not to guidance.

Value Of Needs Identification

The Needs Survey approach has several advantages. Priorities can be established with considerably more objectivity by using tabulations from the Needs Survey instrument. The data make it less likely that subjective opinions, philosophical hassels, or pressures from one individual or group of individuals will thrust program development in a direction which is inconsistent with the needs of students. Through the Needs Survey approach, "armchair" opinions can be challenged or validated and a solid base for program development established. Furthermore, with input from students, parents, and staff, it is difficult to question the credibility of the results. A Needs Survey approach promotes public visibility for the school and the guidance department because of the involvement of students, parents, and staff. Finally, the tangible results of a Needs Survey can contribute to the enthusiasm of the guidance staff since they can be more confident of departmental changes.

Critical Aspects of Student Needs Identification

An important aspect to consider in beginning program development with a Needs Survey is the amount of time involved in development and administration. Tabulation of results can also be a time-consuming process. However, tabulation can be streamlined by using a computer scoring procedure or by careful organization of people and resources at the building level.

The total guidance program being developed may not always be related to the results of the Needs Survey. There are, within a building or school system, certain pressures which necessitate counselor attention and involvement, such as the institutional pressure resulting from student movement from one school level to another, high school graduation requirements, rules and regulations of the school, structure of the curriculum, and the milieu within a building. Each of these pressures requires adjustments on the part of students. These adjustments will directly affect the responsibilities of the counselor.

Another aspect of the systematic needs identification approach in guidance program development is that some needs will not rank high and, as a result, may not receive emphasis in program development. Nevertheless, a student with a low-ranked need should be able to receive assistance from a counselor. The counselor, therefore, cannot entirely base the use of time on the Needs Survey results.

Even though limitations exist to systematic needs identification, the process should be used in guidance program development because of the overall value of such an approach.

Structure Of A Guidance Needs Survey Instrument

The structure of the Needs Survey instrument will facilitate the determination of the counselor's role. The scope of the survey items will directly affect the expectations of counselors, since the items chosen directly reflect the biases of those developing them. In the sample surveys in the appendix beginning on page 57, survey items for later elementary, middle, and senior high schools can be categorized into the following four guidance goal categories:

1. Self-understanding.
2. Decision-making.
3. Interpersonal Relations.
4. Educational and Vocational Development.

For example, when students are asked to respond to whether they have need to "feel more sure of themselves," the item is related to the goal area of *self-understanding.* When they are asked whether they have the need to "learn to make better decisions," the item is directly related to the goal area of *decision-making.* The four listed goal areas have been recommended by the American School Counselors Association (1975) as the areas on which counselors should focus program development. The use of these four guidance goal categories will help insure that program development is balanced and related to the guidance needs of young people. An example of how a survey is divided into goal categories is found on page 69. Specific survey items can be added or deleted depending on the perspective of each school or school district. The sample surveys are intentionally binary in order to facilitate easy scoring. Instead of *Yes* or *No* responses, the surveys can easily be adapted to include responses such as: *Strongly agree, Agree, Disagree,* and *Strongly disagree.*

The Guidance Needs Survey Process: Important Considerations

1. Administrative approval of all needs surveys should be obtained.
2. The survey should reflect a professional effort. Quality paper and professional printing help demonstrate the importance of the survey.
3. Statements divided into categories will help avoid

students answering in a set manner.

4. The survey should avoid open-ended statements in the event interpretation of student responses takes on disproportionate meaning.
5. Test the survey on a small sample of students.
6. The sample surveys can be adapted for use with optical scanning equipment. The development of a survey which can be scored in this manner necessitates careful planning with a commercial company that produces optical scan forms. Most large cities have companies that will assist in the development and printing of these forms. If this technique is used, be certain to test the form prior to administering it to an entire student population.
7. Examine each survey item carefully in light of community acceptance. Some communities are sensitive to answering personal questions.

Administration To Faculty

Administer the Needs Survey to the faculty initially so that they can assist in the administration of student and parent surveys. The simplest method is to administer the survey to faculty in a group, first explaining the purpose of the survey.

Administration To Parents

Prior to actual administration of the parent survey, insert a notice and explanation in the school newspaper and/or local paper. Also utilize other available channels of communication. Distribution of surveys to parents must be planned in advance. Assigning this responsibility to a staff person and a group of students will facilitate and streamline the process. One option to mailing is the distribution of the surveys through individual classrooms.

Teachers can monitor their classes and solicit student assistance for returning the surveys. Contests between rooms, with a reward for the room with the fastest and highest return of surveys, can increase the response rate, especially in elementary and middle schools. An increased response can be attained by distributing the parent survey on the same day as the student survey.

Chapter Four

TABULATING AND INTERPRETING NEEDS SURVEY RESULTS

WHICHEVER tabulation method is used, hand or machine, students can be included in the process. A cooperative arrangement with the mathematics department can save hours of secretarial or counselor time and provide an educational experience in the process.

When the results are tabulated by hand, two persons working together will assure accuracy. A secretary, teacher, or counselor can closely supervise to make sure that the results are reported properly. Tabulating the results in a room where there is little distraction or interruption is important in completing the job both accurately and quickly.

Tabulation

1. Place all the Needs Survey sheets for each grade level together.
2. Use the *Survey Response Tally Sheet* on page 29 and record *Yes* and *No* answers for each question. One person can read while the other records the responses.
3. On the *Survey Response Tally Sheet*, total the responses by grade level. In some instances, results for individual classrooms may be used. For example, in elementary classrooms, the counselor or teacher may want to design classroom activities based on the identified needs of a specific classroom or group.

28

SURVEY RESPONSE TALLY SHEET

ITEM	YES	TOTAL %	NO	TOTAL %
1.				
2.				
3.				
4.				
5.				
6.				
7.				
8.				
9.				
10.				
11.				
12.				
13.				
14.				
15.				
16.				
17.				
18.				
19.				
20.				
21.				
22.				
23.				
24.				
25.				

Ranking

4. Rank responses by completing the *Needs Survey Item Rankings Form* on page 30.

NEEDS SURVEY ITEM RANKINGS

Percentage of Yes Responses

Rank	Item Number	Goal Category	NEEDS SURVEY ITEM As a student, I need to or As a parent, my student needs to or As a staff member, most students at my grade level need to	9th Grade				10th Grade				11th Grade				12th Grade			
				Students	Parents	Staff	Average	Students	Parents	Staff	Average	Students	Parents	Staff	Average	Students	Parents	Staff	Average

NEEDS SURVEY PRIORITIES

Goal Category and Need Statement	SURVEY ITEM Grade:	SURVEY ITEM Grade:	SURVEY ITEM Grade:	SURVEY ITEM Grade:
SELF-UNDERSTANDING				
Priority 1.				
Priority 2.				
Priority 3.				
INTERPERSONAL REACTIONS				
Priority 1.				
Priority 2.				
Priority 3.				
DECISION-MAKING				
Priority 1.				
Priority 2.				
Priority 3.				
EDUCATIONAL-VOCATIONAL DEVELOPMENT				
Priority 1.				
Priority 2.				
Priority 3.				

   5. Using the same form, identify the three survey items responded to with the highest percentages in each goal category (listed on page 25) and place on the *Needs Survey Priority Form,* on page 31.

   6. State each priority survey item by goal category and grade on the *Needs Survey Priority Form.*

Interpretation of Needs Survey Results

The process of interpreting the results of a Needs Survey is more than a statistical analysis of the data. Having one person sit in an office, analyze the data, and then provide an interpretation is not the best way to use the needs survey tabulations. When the tabulations are available, consult with students at the middle and high school levels to determine the meaning behind the priority Needs Survey items. These insights will help the data become relevant and will sensitize the staff to the real needs of the students. Obtaining this feedback will also clarify the perceptions of students at various grade levels. For example, "Learning to make better decisions" could mean something quite different to students at the ninth grade level than to students at the twelfth grade level. It has been stated by Johnson et al. (1961) that characteristics of students vary significantly between age spans; therefore, a developmental interpretation of the needs survey will help clarify these differences.

Obtaining Feedback on the Priorities

Listed below are steps to follow in interpreting the results of the Needs Surveys:

   1. Identify the three survey items in each of the four goal areas which were responded to with the highest percentage of *Yes* responses at each grade level for parents, staff, and students. These items will serve as

a basis for establishing priority needs and insure the development and maintenance of a balanced comprehensive program.

2. Form a small group of students at each grade level in middle and senior high schools. At the elementary level, students are generally in self-contained classrooms. It may be preferable to prioritize student needs by classrooms rather than by grade level. In addition, student feedback regarding perception of surveyed needs may be eliminated at the elementary level.

3. Ask the students to interpret what students mean by their responses to the three priority items in each goal area.

4. Ask the students to determine what students at each grade level want to know or do in order to satisfy or eliminate the need.

5. Ask the students what they appear to be expecting from the counselor at their grade level. Also determing which needs are immediate in nature and which needs are future oriented.

Do not share with students the reactions of students from one grade level to another. Let students express the meaning of their responses, especially if a developmental program is desired.

The following is an example of how a group of middle school students interpreted the meaning of the Needs Survey item, "I need to find out more about what I would like to do in the future about jobs." They thought that students needed the following:

Help in figuring out what classes to take in the future.
Information about areas of work rather than about specific jobs.
Help with some basic ideas of what they could or would like to be in the future.

Write down the student responses to each priority survey

item. It may be necessary for the guidance staff to eliminate some of the responses since, during the dialogue with students, they may deviate from commenting directly about the survey item being considered. Professional judgement must still be used in interpreting what students are indicating by their comments.

Chapter Five

THE PROGRAM

Moving Forward

Reaching For Student Outcomes

HAVING come this far in program development, counselors are aware that, all the while they have
been attending meetings concerned with program development, their working days have been filled with responding
to crises, needs, and other daily activities. Counselors must
now begin to perform activities related to newly stated
student outcomes. In order to do this, it is necessary for the
Guidance Steering Committee to bring order to the work
that has been accomplished and put the work in a format
that can be utilized and understood by others.

Student Outcomes And Activities

Outcome statements will describe the final behavior desired on the part of students as a result of a series of
planned activities. The time at which the behavior will
occur and the students who will do the behaving are also
described. Each guidance service consists of outcome statements and planned activities designed to reach the outcomes, as well as a description of each service. When
developing a guidance program, it is tempting to develop
page upon page of outcome statements. In fact, outcome
statements could be developed for each planned guidance
activity. But a guidance staff cannot perform outcome
statements. It is best to limit the outcome statements of
each guidance service to three. This is simplified by

remembering that an outcome statement is just that, the final behavior desired after a series of planned activities. The systematic development of planned guidance activities designed to reach outcomes is, therefore, as vital as outcome statements.

Writing outcome statements is an exciting challenge. The task is to refer back to the Needs Survey and to write outcome statements directly related to priority items already identified and the comments that students made about them. The pressure to justify the status quo can be very strong at this point in program development. Two basic steps can be followed when writing outcome statements:

First, write all outcome statements before moving further in program development. The guidance department has already identified the priority items on the Needs Survey and has received feedback from students. From that information, outcome statements (Appendix C, page 75) can be developed as shown in these examples:

> Survey item 10, "Learn how to choose high school courses." An outcome statement could be, "By March, tenth grade students will select the courses which they desire to take the next school year."
>
> Survey item 12, "Understand how to choose a career." An outcome statement could be, "By October, tenth grade students will tentatively indicate a career area of interest and the courses needed to prepare for that career."
>
> Survey item 20, "Learn more about my high school records and graduation requirements". An outcome statement could be, "By March, tenth grade students will list the courses they need to complete graduation requirements."

For further assistance in writing outcome statements, the reader is referred to Robert F. Mager's *Preparing In-*

structional Objectives, and *Developing Attitude Toward Learning.*

Second, for each grade level, combine outcome statements into related clusters. For example, all three of the above outcome statements could be related to each other and clustered together in the following order:

a. "By October, tenth grade students will tentatively indicate a career area of interest and the courses needed to prepare for that career."

b. "By March, tenth grade students will list the courses they need to complete graduation requirements."

c. "By March, tenth grade students will select the courses which they desire to take the next school year."

PROGRAMMATIC AND RESPONSE SERVICES. Each guidance department delivers two kinds of services: programmatic and response. Programmatic services consist predominantly of activities that are initiated by the guidance department. Programmatic services are delivered at a specific time or span of time, and their intent is generally to impact all students in a certain grade or category. Services such as these are typically progammatic: Articulation, Orientation, Follow-up, Information, Course Selection, Post-High School Planning, Placement, and Testing.

On the other hand, response services consist predominantly of activities delivered only on demand or immediate need. Response services are delivered throughout the school year, and their intent is most often to impact one student or a small group of students. The following are typically response services: Referral, Staff Consultant, Counseling, and Special Needs. During the process of program development, response services can be overlooked and not included as part of a guidance program. The result is an unbalanced program and may produce a reaction among the guidance staff that something is missing.

DEVELOPING PROGRAMMATIC SERVICES. Outcome statements are not combined into related clusters. Next, take out the work that was accomplished in identifying current services and activities and make as many copies as there are services of the *Service Summary Form* on page 20. Follow these steps:

1. *Using the Service Summary Form,* assign each outcome statement cluster to a service heading such as, Course Selection, Orientation, etc. Additional services may be identified where none now exist. Transfer the outcome statements to the *Service Summary Forms* as in the examples on pages 40 and 41.

2. Identify activities needed to reach each outcome. Examine the activities that have been identified as currently being performed. Eliminate those that will not lead to the stated outcomes, and add others that are necessary. Again, the pressure to justify and maintain the status quo may be intense.

3. Determine the chronological order of the activities needed to achieve the outcomes. State them on the *Service Summary Form* in the place indicated.

4. Identify the materials needed to perform each activity. For many guidance departments, this may be the first time that the need for materials will have been determined in its proper perspective. Too often, materials determine the outcomes and the methods to reach them. Now the activities which were designed to reach specific outcomes will determine which materials are necessary. This may lead many departments to realize that they have few materials that will help them. But now, clear direction exists as to which materials need to be developed or purchased.

DEVELOPING RESPONSE SERVICES. Response services do not easily lend themselves to program development and, as a result, are frequently overlooked and taken for granted. Status quo pressures promote a tendency to respond to all interpersonal relationship needs identified on the Needs

SERVICE SUMMARY FORM

Name of Service   Grade(s):

Description of Service	Service Outcomes

Activities	Month	Materials

NAME OF SERVICE: COURSE SELECTION   GRADE(S): 10

Description	Service Outcomes
The counselor assists students and parents in making decisions regarding course selection and programs of study.	1. Students will indicate a tentative career area of interest and the courses needed to pursue that interest. 2. Students will indicate the courses they need to complete graduation requirements. 3. Students will select courses of interest.

Activities	Month	Materials
1. Review results of previously administered interest inventories with students in small groups or classrooms, and verify the results with them. A. Ask students if they are able to indicate a tentative career direction. B. Review the high school courses related to the career of interest and entrance requirements of educational or training institutions. C. Review graduation requirements with students.	Sept. Oct.	1. Interest Inventory Profile
2. Distribute one copy of the *Student Program Guide* and one course selection sheet to each student in small group classroom. Review the *Guide* and course selection procedure.	Feb. & Mar.	2. *Student Program Guide* & Course Selection Form.
3. Assist students to select their courses for the next school year.		
4. Collect course selection forms from students.		
5. Make appointments with those students needing additional assistance.		5a. Interest Profile 5b. Student Program 5c. Course Selection Form 5d. Student's Cum.
6. Send course selection sheets to data processing center for keypunching.		
7. Upon return from keypunching — verify results with students.		

Surveys in a response fashion. In fact, however, many such needs can be attended to in a programmatic fashion as in

Service Description	Service Outcomes
Planned activities with a group of students for the purpose of assisting them to make an adjustment in school and to form healthy peer relationships.	1. Students will be able to identify and demonstrate three appropriate behaviors for making friends. 2. Based on teacher observations in class and counselor observations in role playing situations, students will demonstrate ways of making friends.

Activities	Month	Materials

1. *First Session:*
  A. Discuss DUSO® Story, *Talks About Friends*
  B. Utilizing Magic Circle, discuss the topic: "A friend I have — why I chose him/her for a friend."
	Oct.
	
	thru
		1A. DUSO Kit

2. *Second Session:* A. Read and discuss the book, *Fuzzies — A Folkfable for all Ages.*	Nov.	2A. *Fuzzies®* Book
3. *Third Session:* A. Make a behavior chart. Identify warm fuzzy feelings (likes) and cold prickly feelings (dislikes)		3A. Tagboard, Magic Marker®, cotton balls

4. *Fourth Session:*
  A. Make warm fuzzies, role play giving them to friends, discuss how it felt to give and to receive.
  B. Review with students the behavior learned.
		4A. Cotton balls

5. *Fifth Session:*
  A. Show and discuss the filmstrip, *Responding.*
  B. Illustrate various methods of responding.
  C. Role play positive and negative behavioral situations regarding making friends. Observe and reinforce appropriate behaviors.
		5A. SRA® Kit
		5B. SRA® Photoboard
		5C. *Conflict Management* Book

6. *Sixth Session:*
  A. Discuss changing behavior, "Things we can do differently to make friends." Make acvity sheet and list different behaviors.
  B. Make behavior modification chart for each child, explicity stating individual goals.
		6A. Activity Sheet
		
		6B. Tagboard

7. *Seventh Session:* A. Show the filmstrip, *Will You be my Friend?* and discuss.		7A. *Getting Along* Kindle Films

8. *Eighth Session:*
  A. Ask students to bring a friend along. Ask them to make up a story and draw a picture relating how they became friends.
  B. Utilizing Magic Circle, discuss "What they like about each other." Review behavior with child and teacher as compared with stated objectives.		

NAME OF SERVICE: REFERRAL   GRADES: ALL

Description	Service Outcomes
The counselor refers students and/or parents to a community or school resource when the need is beyond the range of counselor training or time limitations. When appropriate, the counselor facilitates contact with community resources. The counselor also serves as the school contact person for agencies working with students.	1. Students, parents, and staff will be able to indicate that the counselor is a person who can assist in finding an appropriate community resource. 2. Students or parents who are referred to a community agency will make an appointment with the agency. 3. Referred student and parents will indicate progress, or the lack of it, as a result of the referral.

Activities	Month	Materials
1. Student concern or problem identified which requires help from a specialist more suited to deal with it than is the counselor.	On De- mand	
2. Need for referral is discussed with the student, and student self-referral is encouraged.		
3. Appropriateness of parental involvement discussed with the student.		
4. Referral Resource discussed with the student (and parents) and options, if available, are evaluated.		*Community Resource Guide*
5. Student (parents) decide referral resource desired.		
6. Contact person identified, and method of contact is determined.		
7. Student (parents) makes contact with resource. Where appropriate, counselor inititates contact with resource.		
8. Changes in school schedule and/or school environment implemented if appropriate.		
9. Continued contact with student maintained after referral.		
10. Receives feedback from referral source regarding progress.		

the example on page 41. This sample depicts group activities which center on appropriate behaviors for making friends.

If a balanced program is to exist, response services are important. While counselors are out of their offices delivering planned programmatic services, day-to-day student adjustment concerns and crises continue to occur in every school building. Referrals continue to be received from teachers, and students continue to make appointments to see their counselors. Any effort at program development must take this into account or counselors may feel overwhelmed, and the program may not be delivered.

The same format used to develop programmatic services can be used to develop response services. Each can be included on a *Service Summary Form.* For example, certain procedures or activities are generally followed when students and/or parents are referred to a community resource. These activities are listed in the *Activities* portion of the *Service Summary Form.* There are also student outcomes that can be developed. For both student outcomes and activities, refer to the example on page 42.

Similarly, when students initiate a contact with a counselor for counseling, there are procedures that are generally followed within a guidance department. Program development provides the opportunity to formalize these procedures. The *Activity* portion of the *Service Summary Form* should include all the steps starting with a student making an appointment with a counselor through the receipt of feedback from the student. Again, a student outcome cluster such as this can be developed:

1. "Students will be able to indicate that the counselor is a person who is trained to assist with adjustment concerns, concerns about relationships with others, and concerns about self."
2. "As a result of the counseling contact(s), students will indicate that the situation of concern has improved."

3. "Ten percent of the student body will make appointments with counselors for the purpose of counseling."

Guidance Calendar Development

A complete collection of services, each with its own calendar of activities, has been developed by the Guidance Steering Committee. This format will assist counselors assigned to each service, and also will assist administrators, supervisors, or head counselors to coordinate the delivery of each guidance service. But, in order to coordinate the delivery of the entire guidance program, an additional format is necessary. Refer to the *Calendar Form* on page 45. Make several copies, and do the following:

First, list programmatic activities of all services in chronological order by month. A perfect listing of chronological order is not necessary. A listing of activities by month, however, will allow an administrator to review the implementation of the program at least monthly.

Second, indicate the person(s) responsible for delivering each activity. Time needed to deliver each activity should be a consideration so that a given counselor does not become overloaded. When more activities are scheduled to be performed at a particular time than can be delivered, alternative times, activities, or assistance may be planned.

Organizing the Guidance Program Handbook

The format followed in putting the program on paper will have a direct effect on how well the program will be delivered. A *Service Summary Form* describing each service, and a guidance calendar have been developed. The format for organizing the guidance program handbook should be determined by how well it will facilitate program delivery and by its communication possibilities to

GUIDANCE SERVICES FOR THE MONTH OF _____

TASKS TO BE COMPLETED (Chronological Order)	SERVICE	GRADE	ASSIGNED	NOT ASSIGNED	COUNSELOR(S) RESPONSIBLE	DATE COMPLETE

various publics. The use of a loose-leaf notebook will facilitate program organization. A recommended format which will facilitate and communicate is as follows:

First, divide the services into grade levels. Needs and services which distinguish between grade levels have already been identified and developed. There will be many services which will duplicate each other from one grade level to another, but in many buildings, counselors are assigned by grade level. Therefore, if the same service with the same activities is listed two or three times under two or more separate grade levels, it really is not a duplication. When parents or others desire to become familiar with the guidance program, most are interested in only one grade level and how the guidance program will impact students at that particular level.

Second, divide the services at each grade level into the three areas generally accepted for guidance programs: Personal-Social Services, Educational Services, and Career Services; or, the four guidance goal areas described in Chapter Three: Self-understanding, Decision-making, Interpersonal Relations, and Educational and Vocational Development. There are times when a few services will overlap these categories. An example is the Course Selection Service if career activities are infused. The decision can be made to put the service into either the Educational or Career Services category.

Third, place a table of contents at the beginning of the booklet and before each grade level. If budget will allow, services in each grade level may be printed with a separate color. An illustration of these three steps is on page 47. The illustration is for grades seven through twelve. A guidance program that serves kindergarten through grade twelve can be divided into two or three separate handbooks, one for elementary and one for secondary schools or one each for elementary, middle, and senior high schools.

Fourth, the guidance calendar may be placed at the front of the guidance booklet.

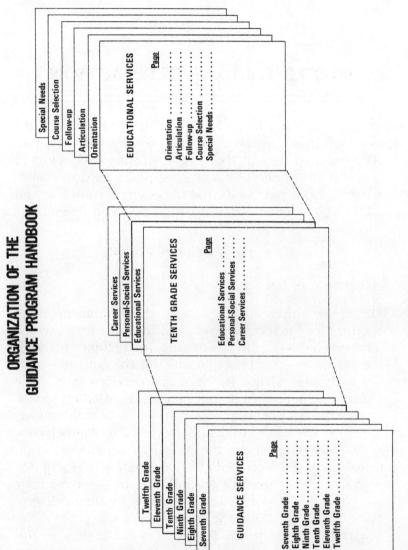

Figure 1.

Chapter Six

PUTTING PLANS INTO ACTION

PERFORMING planned activities is the next step in the process of program development. Program delivery is so natural that it is frequently overlooked in terms of planning. The process of performing the developed program puts to the test the extent of counselor and administrator commitment to what has been developed.

Assigning Responsibilities

Assignment of Services

Program initiation begins with the assignment of responsibility for specific services to individual counselors. This can be accomplished at a guidance staff meeting with the person or persons responsible for the guidance staff. Certainly, the talents, interests, and experiences of individual staff members should be considered when service responsibilities are assigned. Additional considerations include the size of the student body, previous counselor responsibilities, the size of the guidance staff, and the scope of several of the developed guidance services. The scope of several of the services will generally require that more than one counselor be assigned responsibility for their delivery. For example, the Course Selection Service will probably be delivered by the entire guidance staff. Some services, on the other hand, will be delivered more effectively if assigned to only one counselor.

If guidance responsibilities are divided into specialties, such as one counselor for career counseling, one for college planning, etc., much duplication of counselor activities may occur. As a result, students frequently must be referred from one counselor to another in order to receive specialized services. This may be perceived by students as inefficient and impersonal. In addition, when guidance responsibilities are divided into specialties, counselor differences, rather than similarities, may be perceived by students, administrators, and counselors. This may result in low morale coupled with communication problems within the guidance staff.

Job Description

Develop an overall job description for counselors. The job description should include the purpose of the position and the major responsibilities of counselors. The purpose of the position should include reference to meeting the identified priority needs of students. The major responsibilities are a listing of the descriptions of the developed services. Approval of this job description by the administration and/or the board of education is critical.

Management

After services have been assigned to counselors, a management system is important. Part of this system is the establishment of regularly scheduled meetings. The newly developed guidance calendar serves as an excellent management tool. It serves as a regular agenda item for guidance staff meetings with administrators or with counselors within a department. Planning through the use of a calendar makes a department's activities visible and public. Management of a guidance staff has traditionally been considered a problem for many building administrators because the counselor's function is often nebulous. Administrators generally appreciate the direction a well-developed guidance calendar provides. This calendar keeps the administrator constantly aware of day-to-day responsibilities of individual members of the guidance staff. This factor alone will tend to inhibit the assignment of additional responsibilities to counselors.

In performing developed services, counselors are frequently away from their offices in order to meet with groups of students or to be in classrooms. If a school has several counselors in a guidance suite, coordination of counselor movement is necessary in order to perform response activities such as crisis counseling. So that the movement of students to the guidance office for services can continue, at least one guidance staff member should always be available. Activities should be planned in advance and the guidance secretary informed. Appointments can then be made smoothly without conflicting with scheduled activities.

Counselors in many school districts are placed in offices located separately around the school building with little or no secretarial services. In this case, each counselor may want to consider posting daily or weekly guidance activity schedules on their individual office doors or in a visible place near their offices. When the counselor is not available, students will know why and will be able to sign up for appointments.

Assignment of services and the expectation that counselors perform planned activities cannot be divorced from staffing considerations. Sufficient staff to deliver planned activities is as vital as the planning; otherwise, the quality of the service delivery will diminish. As ratios of students to counselors increase, the ability of the guidance staff to initiate planned activities diminishes proportionately unless expectations are drastically altered.

Program Refinement — Internal Review

After a few months of working with the new program,

the question will be raised as to whether the outcomes are being achieved by the performance of the planned activities. A conflict quickly arises. Should the guidance staff expend energy during the first year of program delivery to develop ways of finding evidence of program success, or should staff expend its energy making certain the program is delivered and the delivery refined? The energy and time that it will take to execute and refine the program during the first year can supercede the assessment of outcomes unless the school district is willing to contract with an evaluator who is not a member of the guidance department. In addition, the development of materials which communicate the program to students, parents, teachers, and administrators is vitally important during the first year of the program.

The process of program delivery and program communication are valuable topics of discussion at guidance staff meetings. Each step of program delivery is best assessed if it is examined as it occurs. The ease of performing service activities, the coordination of these activities, and whether or not the activities appear to be related to the student outcomes should be assessed constantly. The activities of each service can be easily assessed if counselors write notes on their personal copies of the program. The Guidance Steering Committee should continue to meet periodically to assess recommendations to change, add, or delete service activities.

Another helpful tool for internal review is the *Weekly Log* (shown on page 52) and *Monthly Summary* (page 53). These tools can help a department review its balance of service delivery. Are the goals of the guidance department being delivered to students in a balanced way, or is disproportionate energy being expended in only one or two areas? Is there a balance between programmed activities and response activities? For example, can students make appointments easily?

WEEKLY LOG						
WEEK OF_____ COUNSELOR_____ SCHOOL_____						
REASON FOR CONTACT	MON	TUES	WED	THUR	FRI	TOTAL
1. Number of crisis or emergency contacts						
2. Number of contacts for Personal-Social Services						
3. Number of contacts for Educational Services						
4. Number of contacts for Career Services						
5. Number of referrals to community agencies						
6. Number of contacts with community agencies						
7. Number of referrals to school resources						
8. Number of group counseling sessions						
9. Number of group guidance sessions						
10. Number of contacts with parents						
11. Number of home visitations						
12. Number of contacts with teachers re: Students						
13. Number of staff conferences re teachers, administrators, etc.						
14. Number of referrals from teachers, administrators, etc.						
15. Other						
16. Other						
Additional Requests by administrators and others:						

Program evaluation in terms of outcome achievement can be accomplished during the second year of program delivery. Criterion-reference items can be developed to measure the degree of attainment of student outcomes. An example of an outcome statement is, "By March, tenth

---

MONTHLY SUMMARY

MONTH OF_____ COUNSELOR_____ SCHOOL_____

1. Number of crisis or emergency contacts . . . . _____
2. Number of contacts for Personal-Social Counseling . . . . . . _____
3. Number of contacts for Educational Planning . . . . _____
4. Number of contacts for Career Counseling . . . . _____
5. Number of referrals to community agencies . . . . _____
6. Number of contacts with community agencies . . . . _____
7. Number of referrals to school resources . . . . _____
8. Number of group counseling sessions . . . . _____
9. Number of group guidance sessions . . . . _____
10. Number of contacts with parents . . . . _____
11. Number of home visitations . . . . _____
12. Number of contacts with teachers re students . . . . _____
13. Number of staff conferences re students . . . . _____
14. Number of referrals from teachers, etc. . . . . _____
15. Other . . . . _____
16. Other . . . . _____

Additional Requests by administrators and others:

graders will be able to state the number of credits required for graduation." An evaluation item could be, "How many credits are required to graduate?"

Staff Training

One of the main reasons new programs often fail is the lack of appropriate training for those working in the program. Training programs should be ongoing and related to the needs of the staff as they pertain to the developed guidance program. Program development leads to the identification of skills needed to perform the activities designed to reach program outcomes. For example, activities may require skills in working with groups. Program development will help identify the skills and approaches needed.

When reviewing or determining in-service programs for counselors, it is important to select only those in-service programs which will assist counselors in gaining skills to improve the delivery of planned activities. This is not to say that additional inservice programs should be avoided in areas such as legal requirements, new programs, or other needed informational topics. Part of the follow-up of any in-service activity should be a discussion regarding how the new skills or information can be infused into the guidance program.

Guidance Materials

It has already been mentioned that developing a guidance program gives direction to the identification of needed materials. Most guidance departments have many materials on hand; but after their initial enthusiasm for materials, counselors often discontinue their use. This is generally because the materials determine the purpose, the outcomes, and the activities. Program development gives the guidance department the opportunity to review materials on hand to determine if all or parts can be utilized to reach newly stated outcomes. If the use of certain materials is included on the *Service Summary Form* as they are needed to perform prescribed activities, their regular use will be guaranteed.

Program development provides a base from which to review additional materials for purchase. If a certain material will assist the guidance department in achieving its outcomes and if the material will fit into the work loads and timelines already determined, its trial review could be considered. If not, purchase of the material is not advisable.

Conclusion

When viewing the total process of guidance program development, it may seem overwhelming. When viewed as a step-by-step process that will take at least one school year to develop and another to implement, guidance program development is feasible, manageable, and exciting. As the process nears completion, those involved in program development will realize how uncomplicated and smooth the process can be.

ELEMENTARY NEEDS SURVEYS

Directions for the Administration of the
Early Elementary Guidance Needs Survey

Dear Teacher:

Below are directions for the administration of a survey of guidance needs to be given on (day), (date). The purpose of the survey is to identify the guidance needs of students in your classroom. The results will be used to assist in the development of our guidance program.

Before the guidance needs survey forms are distributed to the students, read aloud the directions which are in italics.

"For the next few minutes, we are going to play a little game together. I would like you to show me how you look when you feel happy."

Let the students express their happy faces, and show them a drawing of a happy face.

"Very good! Now show me how you look when you feel sad."

Let the students express their sad faces, and show them a drawing of a sad face. Then say:

I am going to pass out three things to each of you: a piece of paper with happy and sad faces on it, and a crayon. You will also be given a plain piece of paper. Please do not write on any of the papers until I tell you."

Pass out the paper and crayons. Then say:

"Print your name on the top line. Place your plain piece of paper on top of your paper with the faces on it." (Show them how to do this.) *"Remember to color in only one face for each question."*

Read one item at a time, making sure students are coloring in only one face.

"Now move your blank paper down to the picture of the star."

Make sure they have done this correctly. Identify each survey item by the picture in front of each item, and proceed to move from item to item until the survey is completed.

Return the completed surveys to the guidance office.

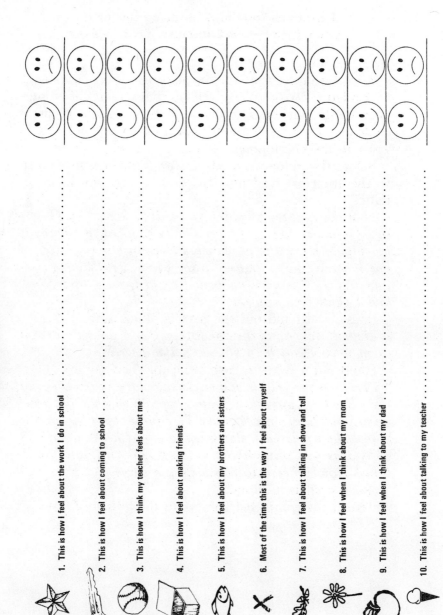

EARLY ELEMENTARY NEEDS SURVEY

1. This is how I feel about the work I do in school

2. This is how I feel about coming to school

3. This is how I think my teacher feels about me

4. This is how I feel about making friends

5. This is how I feel about my brothers and sisters

6. Most of the time this is the way I feel about myself

7. This is how I feel about talking in show and tell

8. This is how I feel when I think about my mom

9. This is how I feel when I think about my dad

10. This is how I feel about talking to my teacher

Directions for the Administration of the
Later Elementary Guidance Needs Survey

Dear Teacher:

Below are directions for the administration of a survey of guidance needs to be given on (day), (date). The purpose of the survey is to identify the guidance needs of students in your classroom. The results will be used to assist in the development of our guidance program.

Before the guidance needs survey forms are distributed to the students, read aloud the directions which are in italics.

"For the next ten minutes, you will be asked to take part in a Guidance Needs Survey. The purpose of the survey is to help improve the guidance and counseling services of our school. Your responses to the survey will be kept confidential. If you have no pencil or pen, raise your hand, and I shall lend you one."

Pause, and hand out the pencils. Then say:

"I shall now hand out the forms. Please do not write on them until I can help you with the directions."

Hand out a form to each student. Then say:

"Look at the grades, and circle your present grade . . . In the survey, we are asking you what you think about your needs. The only correct answers are those that are right for you. I shall read each statement to you. Check either YES or NO as you think about yourself. Are there any questions? Now proceed to complete the survey."

(Read each item aloud.)

Return the completed surveys to the guidance office.

Later Elementary Student Needs Survey

Circle your grade: 4   5   6   **YES NO**

1. I'm happy most of the time .... ___ ___
2. When given a choice, I can make decisions easily .... ___ ___
3. I get along well with my father .... ___ ___
4. Most of the time, I would rather be alone than play with others .... ___ ___
5. My feelings are easily hurt .... ___ ___
6. I often bite my nails .... ___ ___
7. My parents feel I can do things well ... ___ ___
8. I get along well with other kids .... ___ ___
9. I get mad very easily .... ___ ___
10. The teacher always tells me to talk louder in class .... ___ ___
11. I have an easy time making friends .... ___ ___
12. I think other kids like me .... ___ ___
13. I like school .... ___ ___
14. I am sometimes a show-off in class .... ___ ___
15. I have a hard time keeping my mind on my school work .... ___ ___
16. I miss a lot of days from school .... ___ ___
17. I get along well with my teacher ...... ___ ___
18. I do well on my school work .... ___ ___
19. I have nightmares at least two times a week .... ___ ___
20. I get along well with my mother ...... ___ ___
21. I have trouble getting along with my brothers or sisters .... ___ ___
22. I get into a lot of hitting fights .... ___ ___

Thank You!

Elementary Student Needs Survey
(Parents)

Dear Parent:

We would like your help in an important project to improve the guidance and counseling program of our school. As a first step, we are asking students, parents, and staff to complete this survey. If you have more than one student in our school, please fill out one for each. Your help is important to the success of this project.

Circle the grade of your son or daughter: K 1 2 3 4 5 6

Show how important each need is to you by checking the column which shows what you think.

My child: **YES NO**

1. Is happy most of the time ....   ___ ___
2. Can make decisions easily when given a choice ....   ___ ___
3. Can get along with his/her father .....   ___ ___
4. Would rather be alone than play with others most of the time ....   ___ ___
5. Has his/her feelings easily hurt........   ___ ___
6. Often bites his/her nails ....   ___ ___
7. Has nightmares at least two times a week.................................   ___ ___
8. Misses a lot of days from school.......   ___ ___

My youngster:

9. Gets mad very easily...................   ___ ___
10. Needs to talk louder in class ....   ___ ___
11. Has an easy time making friends ......   ___ ___
12. Thinks other kids like her or him .....   ___ ___
13. Likes school ....   ___ ___

14. Is sometimes a show-off in class .... ___ ___
15. Has a hard time keeping his or her mind on school work........................ ___ ___

As a parent, I think my child:

16. Gets along well with other kids .... ___ ___
17. Gets along well with his/her teacher ... ___ ___
18. Does well in school work .... ___ ___
19. Gets along well with his/her mother... ___ ___
20. Can do things well .... ___ ___
21. Has trouble getting along with brothers or sisters................................ ___ ___
22. Gets into a lot of hitting fights .... ___ ___

Thank you!

Elementary Student Needs Survey

(Staff)

Dear Staff Member:

We would like your help in an important project to improve the guidance and counseling program of our school. As a first step, we are asking students, parents, and staff to complete this survey. Your help is important to the success of this project.

Circle the grade level you teach: K 1 2 3 4 5 6

Show how important each is to you by checking the column which shows what you think.

Most children I work with: **YES NO**

1. Are happy most of the time .... ___ ___
2. Can make decisions easily when given a choice .... ___ ___
3. Can get along well with their fathers .. ___ ___
4. Would rather be alone than play with others most of the time .... ___ ___
5. Have their feelings easily hurt .... ___ ___
6. Often bite their nails .... ___ ___
7. Have nightmares at least two times a week................................. ___ ___
8. Miss a lot of days from school .... ___ ___

Most youngsters at my grade:

9. Get mad very easily.................... ___ ___
10. Need to talk louder in class .... ___ ___
11. Have an easy time making friends ..... ___ ___
12. Think other kids like them .... ___ ___

13. Like school .... ___ ___
14. Sometimes show-off in class .... ___ ___
15. Have a hard time keeping their minds on school work .... ___ ___

Most students at my grade level:

16. Get along well with other kids .... ___ ___
17. Get along well with their teacher ...... ___ ___
18. Do well with school work .... ___ ___
19. Get along well with their mothers ..... ___ ___
20. Can do things well .... ___ ___
21. Have trouble getting along with brothers or sisters .... ___ ___
22. Get into a lot of hitting fights .... ___ ___

Thank you!

MIDDLE SCHOOL NEEDS SURVEYS

Directions for the Administration of the Middle School Guidance Needs Survey

Dear Teacher:

Below are directions for the administration of a survey of guidance needs to be given on (day), (date). The purpose of the survey is to identify the guidance needs of students in your classroom. The results will be used to assist in the development of our guidance program.

Before the guidance needs survey forms are passed out to the students, read the following aloud:

"For the next ten minutes, you will be asked to take part in a Guidance Needs Survey. The purpose of the survey is to help improve the guidance and counseling services of our school. Your responses to the survey will be kept confidential. if you have no pen or pencil, raise your hand, and I shall lend you one."

Pause, and hand out pencils. Then say:

"I shall now hand out the forms. Please do not write on them until I can help you with the directions."

Hand out a form to each student. Then say:

"Look at the grades and circle your present grade . . . In the survey, we are asking you what you think about your needs. The only correct answers are those that are right for you. I shall read each survey item to you. Check either YES or NO as you think about yourself. Are there any questions?"

Proceed to read each survey item to the students.

Middle School Student Needs Survey

Circle your grade: 6 7 8 9

Show how important each need is to you by checking the column which shows what you think.

As a student, I need to: YES NO

1. Feel more sure (confident) of myself ...   ____ ____
2. Learn how to study better.............   ____ ____
3. Find out about what I would like to do in
   the future about jobs ....   ____ ____
4. Talk with teachers and have them understand me as a person ....   ____ ____
5. Be myself rather than try to be what
   someone else wants me to be ....   ____ ____
6. Understand my interests...............   ____ ____
7. Solve my personal problems...........   ____ ____

I need to:

8. Learn to make better decisions ....   ____ ____
9. Get along better with my parents......   ____ ____
10. Find out about choosing high school
    courses...............................   ____ ____
11. Understand what to do about drugs or
    alcohol ....   ____ ____
12. Understand how to choose a career ....   ____ ____
13. Feel more relaxed in school ....   ____ ____

It is important for me to:

14. Learn to keep from putting things off
    until the last minute.................   ____ ____

15. Get along better with my sisters and brothers............................ —— ——
16. Find out what I am good at doing .... —— ——
17. Learn how to make good use of my free time .... —— ——
18. Learn to talk with others .... —— ——
19. Learn to get along better with the opposite sex .... —— ——

I need to:

20. Learn how to become more active in school activities .... —— ——
21. Learn to choose friends .... —— ——
22. Learn to get along better with kids at school .... —— ——
23. Find out more about choosing Middle School courses...................... —— ——
24. Find out about further training and education .... —— ——

Thank you!

Needs Statements and Their Related Goal Categories
Middle School

Self-understanding
1. Feel more sure (confident) of myself.
5. Be myself rather than try to be what someone else wants me to be.
6. Understand my interests.
13. Feel more relaxed in school.

Decision-making
7. Solve my personal problems.
8. Learn to make better decisions.
10. Find out about choosing high school courses.
11. Understand what to do about drugs or alcohol.
12. Understand how to choose a career.
14. Learn to keep from putting things off until the last minute.
17. Learn how to make good use of my free time.
21. Learn to choose friends.
23. Find out more about choosing middle school courses.

Interpersonal Relations
4. Talk with teachers and have them understand me as a person.
9. Get along better with my parents.
15. Get along better with my sisters and brothers.
18. Learn to talk with others.
19. Learn to get along better with the opposite sex.
22. Learn to get along better with kids at school.

Educational and Vocational Development
2. Learn how to study better.
3. Find out about what I would like to do in the future about jobs.
20. Learn how to become more active in school activities.
24. Find out about further training and education.

Middle School Student Needs Survey
(Parents)

Dear Parent:

We would like your help in an important project to improve the guidance and counseling program of our school. As a first step in our project, we are asking students, parents, and staff to complete this survey. If you have more than one student in our school, please fill out one for each. Your help is important to the success of this project.

Circle the grade of your son or daughter: 6 7 8 9

Show how important each need is to you by checking the column which shows what you think.

My student needs to: YES   NO

1. Feel more sure (confident) of himself/ herself .... ___ ___
2. Learn how to study better............. ___ ___
3. Find out about what to do in the future about jobs .... ___ ___
4. Talk with teachers and have teachers understand him/her as a person .... ___ ___
5. Be himself/herself rather than try to be what someone else wants him/her to be .... ___ ___
6. Understand his/her interests .... ___ ___
7. Solve his or her personal problems .... ___ ___

My daughter/son needs to:

8. Learn to make better decisions .... ___ ___
9. Get along better with parents .... ___ ___

10. Find out about choosing high school courses............................... ___ ___
11. Understand what to do about drugs or alcohol .... ___ ___
12. Understand how to choose a career .... ___ ___
13. Feel more relaxed in school .... ___ ___

It is important for my son or daughter to:

14. Learn to keep from putting things off until the last minute................. ___ ___
15. Get along better with sisters and brothers............................ ___ ___
16. Find out what he/she is good at doing............................... ___ ___
17. Learn how to make good use of free time .... ___ ___
18. Learn to talk with others .... ___ ___
19. Learn to get along better with the opposite sex .... ___ ___

He/she needs to:

20. Become more active in school activities .... ___ ___
21. Learn to choose friends .... ___ ___
22. Learn to get along better with kids in school .... ___ ___
23. Find out more about choosing middle school courses .... ___ ___
24. Find out about further training and education .... ___ ___

Thank you!

Middle School Student Needs Survey
(Staff)

Dear Staff Member:

We would like your help in an important project to improve our school's guidance and counseling program. As a first step in our project, we are asking students, parents, and staff to complete this survey. Your help is important to the success of this project.

Circle the grade level you teach: 6 7 8 9

(If you are teaching classes which serve students from different grades, indicate the grade which reflects the highest percentage of your students).

Show how important each need is to you by checking the column which shows what you think.

Most students at my grade level need to: YES NO

1. Feel more sure (confident) of themselves .... ___ ___
2. Learn how to study better .... ___ ___
3. Find out what to do in the future about jobs .... ___ ___
4. Talk with teachers and have them understand them as persons .... ___ ___
5. Be themselves rather than trying to be what someone else wants them to be... ___ ___
6. Understand their interests .... ___ ___
7. Solve their personal problems .... ___ ___

At my grade level, most students need to:

8. Learn to make better decisions .... ___ ___
9. Get along better with their parents .... ___ ___

10. Find out about choosing high school courses.................................. ___ ___
11. Understand what to do about drugs or alcohol .... ___ ___
12. Understand how to choose a career .... ___ ___
13. Feel more relaxed in school .... ___ ___

It is important for most students at my grade level to:

14. Learn to keep from putting things off until the last minute.................. ___ ___
15. Get along better with their sisters and brothers.............................. ___ ___
16. Find out what they are good at doing.................................. ___ ___
17. Learn how to make good use of their free time .... ___ ___
18. Learn to talk with others .... ___ ___
19. Learn to get along better with the opposite sex .... ___ ___

Most students at my grade level need to:

20. Become more active in school activities .... ___ ___
21. Learn to choose friends .... ___ ___
22. Learn to get along better with kids at school .... ___ ___
23. Find out more about choosing middle school courses .... ___ ___
24. Find out about further training and education .... ___ ___

Thank you!

HIGH SCHOOL NEEDS SURVEYS

Directions for the Administration of the
High School Guidance Needs Survey

Before the needs survey forms are passed out to the students, read the following aloud:

"For the next ten minutes, you will be asked to take part in a Guidance Needs Survey. The purpose of the survey is to help improve the guidance and counseling services of our school. Your responses to the survey will be kept confidential. If you have no pencil or pen, raise your hand, and I shall lend you one."

Pause, and hand out pencils. Then say:

"I shall now hand out the forms. Please do not write on them until I can help you with the directions."

Hand out a form to each student. Then say:

"Look at the grades, and circle your present grade . . . In the survey, we are asking you what you think about your needs. The only correct answers are those that are right for you. There is no exact time limit; however, we do ask that you answer all questions carefully and quickly. Read each statement and check either YES or NO as you think about yourself. When you are finished, wait quietly, and we shall collect the surveys. Are there any questions? . . . Go ahead and begin."

High School Student Needs Survey

Circle your grade: 9 10 11 12

Show how important each need is to you by checking the column which shows what you think.

As a student I need to: YES NO

1. Feel more sure (confident) of myself ...   ____ ____
2. Learn how to study better............   ____ ____
3. Find out about what I would like to do in
   the future about jobs ....   ____ ____
4. Talk with teachers and have them understand me as a person ....   ____ ____
5. Be myself rather than try to be what
   someone else wants me to be..........   ____ ____
6. Understand my interests..............   ____ ____
7. Solve my personal problems...........   ____ ____

I need to:

8. Learn to make better decisions ....   ____ ____
9. Get along better with my parents......   ____ ____
10. Find out more about choosing high
    school courses ....   ____ ____
11. Understand what to do about drugs or
    alcohol ....   ____ ____
12. Understand how to choose a career ....   ____ ____
13. Feel more relaxed in school ....   ____ ____

It is important for me to:

14. Learn to keep from putting things off
    until the last minute.................   ____ ____

15. Get along better with my brothers and sisters .... ___ ___
16. Find out what I am good at doing .... ___ ___
17. Learn to make good use of my free time .... ___ ___
18. Learn to talk with others .... ___ ___
19. Learn to get along better with the opposite sex .... ___ ___
20. Learn more about my high school records and graduation requirements .... ___ ___

I need to:

21. Understand how to find a job after graduation .... ___ ___
22. Become more active in school activities .... ___ ___
23. Learn how to choose friends .... ___ ___
24. Learn to get along better with friends at school .... ___ ___
25. Find out about further training or education .... ___ ___

Thank you!

High School Student Needs Survey
(Parents)

Dear Parent:

We would like your help in an important project to improve the guidance and counseling program of our school. As a first step in our project, we are asking students, parents, and staff to complete this survey. If you have more than one student in our school, please fill out one survey for each. Your help is important to the success of this project.

Circle the grade of your son or daughter: 9 10 11 12

Show how important each need is to you by checking the column which shows what you think.

As a parent, my student needs to: YES NO

1. Feel more sure (confident) of himself/ herself .... ___ ___
2. Learn how to study better............. ___ ___
3. Find out about what he/she would like to do in the future about jobs .... ___ ___
4. Talk with teachers and have teachers understand him/her as a person.......... ___ ___
5. Be himself/herself rather than try to be what someone else wants him/her to be .... ___ ___
6. Understand his/her interests .... ___ ___
7. Solve her or his personal problems .... ___ ___

My son/daughter needs to:

8. Learn to make better decisions .... ___ ___
9. Learn to get along better with parents .... ___ ___

10. Learn how to choose high school courses.............................. ___ ___
11. Understand what to do about drugs or alcohol .... ___ ___
12. Understand how to choose a career .... ___ ___
13. Feel more relaxed in school .... ___ ___

It is important for my son/daughter to:

14. Learn to keep from putting things off until the last minute................. ___ ___
15. Get along better with sisters and brothers.............................. ___ ___
16. Find out what he/she is good at doing................................. ___ ___
17. Learn how to make good use of free time .... ___ ___
18. Learn to talk with others .... ___ ___
19. Learn to get along better with the opposite sex .... ___ ___
20. Learn more about his/her high school records and graduation requirements ... ___ ___

My son/daughter needs to:

21. Understand how to find a job after graduation .... ___ ___
22. Become more active in school activities .... ___ ___
23. Learn how to choose friends .... ___ ___
24. Learn to get along better with kids at school .... ___ ___
25. Find out about further training or education .... ___ ___

Thank you!

High School Student Needs Survey
(Staff)

Dear Staff Member:

We would like your help in an important project to improve our school's guidance and counseling program. As a first step in our project, we are asking students, parents, and staff to complete this survey. Your help is important to the success of this project.

Circle the grade level you teach: 9   10   11   12

(If you are teaching classes which serve students from different grades, indicate the grade which reflects the highest percentage of your students.)

Show how important each need is to you by checking the column which shows what you think.

Most students at my grade level need to: YES   NO

1. Feel more sure (confident) of themselves   ____ ____
2. Learn how to study better.............   ____ ____
3. Find out about what they would like to do in the future about jobs...............   ____ ____
4. Talk with teachers and have them understand them as persons ....   ____ ____
5. Be themselves rather than try to be what someone else wants them to be ....   ____ ____
6. Understand their interests ....   ____ ____
7. Solve their personal problems ....   ____ ____

At my grade level most students need to:

8. Learn to make better decisions ....   ____ ____
9. Get along better with their parents ....   ____ ____

10. Learn how to choose high school courses.............................. ___ ___
11. Understand what to do about drugs and alcohol .... ___ ___
12. Understand how to choose a career .... ___ ___
13. Feel more relaxed in school .... ___ ___

It is important for most students at my grade level to:

14. Learn to keep from putting things off until the last minute................. ___ ___
15. Get along better with their sisters and brothers............................ ___ ___
16. Find out about what they are good at doing................................ ___ ___
17. Learn how to make good use of their free time .... ___ ___
18. Learn to talk with others .... ___ ___
19. Learn to get along better with the opposite sex .... ___ ___
20. Learn more about their high school requirements .... ___ ___

Most students at my grade level need to:

21. Understand how to find a job after graduation .... ___ ___
22. Become more active in school activities.................................. ___ ___
23. Learn how to choose friends .... ___ ___
24. Learn to get along better with kids at school .... ___ ___
25. Find out about further training or education .... ___ ___

Thank you!

BIBLIOGRAPHY

1. Hays, Donald G. and Linn, Joan K.: *Needs Assessment! Who Needs It?* Washington, D.C., American School Counselors Association, 1977.
2. Jacobsen, Thomas J. and Mitchell, Anita: How to Develop a District Master Plan for Career Guidance and Counseling. *The Vocational Guidance Quarterly, 25*:195-202, 1977.
3. Johnson, Walter F., Stefflre, Buford, and Edefelt, Roy D.: *Pupil Personnel and Guidance Services.* New York, McGraw, 1961.
4. Kaufman, R. A. and English, F. W.: *A Guide to Improve School District Management.* Virginia, American Association of School Administrators, 1976.
5. Mager, Robert F.: *Developing Attitude Toward Learning.* Palo Alto, CA, Fearon, 1968.
6. Mager, Robert F.: *Preparing Instructional Objectives.* Palo Alto, CA, Fearon, 1972.
7. Michigan School Counselors Association: *Reaction to Action Guidance.* Michigan School Counselors Association, 1974.
8. Mitchell, Anita M. and Saun, James A.: *California Personnel and Guidance Association Monograph.* No. 4, 1972.
9. American School Counselors Association: Counseling and Guidance Programs: Staffing and Responsibilities. *Newsletter,* October 27, 1975.
10. Schmidt, James C. and White, Jack: Middle to Model: The Process of Guidance Program Self Renewal. *Michigan Personnel and Guidance Journal, 5*:7-13, 1974.
11. Shaw, Mervell C.: The Development of Counseling Programs: Priorities, Progress, and Professionalism. *The Personnel and Guidance Journal, 55*:339-345, 1977.
12. Wiggins, James D.: *Tested Practices: Organizing a School Counseling Program.* Washington, D.C., National Vocational Guidance Association, 1974.

INDEX